BUKOWSKI
FOR BEGINNERS®

CARLOS POLIMENI

ILLUSTRATIONS BY
MIGUEL REP

FOR BEGINNERS®

For Beginners LLC
155 Main Street, Suite 211
Danbury, CT 06810 USA
www.forbeginnersbooks.com

.

A For Beginners® Documentary Comic Book
Originally published by Writers and Readers, Inc.
Copyright © 2000

Cataloging-in-Publication information is available from the
Library of Congress.

ISBN # 978-1-939994-37-0 Trade

Manufactured in the United States of America

For Beginners® and Beginners Documentary Comic Books®
are published by For Beginners LLC.

First Edition

10 9 8 7 6 5 4 3 2 1

Contents

1 Kindergarten

'I am not primarily a poet, I hate god gooey damned people poets messing the smears of their lives against the sniveling world...what I write, is only one tenth of myself—the other 9/to hell tenths are looking over the edge of a cliff down into the sea of rock and wringing swirl and cheap damnation...'

Though Henry Charles Bukowski has achieved 'cult' status as a writer, and acquired a world-wide following, he is rarely ranked amongst the literary greats by academics and critics. Bukowski, in their eyes, remains a controversial writer.

Perhaps the lack of establishment recognition is due partly to Bukowski's decadent, dangerous image, his refusal to conform to political correctness (I *am* the outsider') and partly to the fact that he was born in Germany.

And experts in German literature, consider Bukowski to be an American writer. Not surprising, since he wrote only in English and, like an Olympian god, ignored whatever was happening in the rest of the world. He was concerned primarily with his own world, his own private hell: 'I have always been one of those people who do everything wrong. This is essentially because I am not involved in the march'.

His father, Henry Bukowski, found himself in Germany as an enlisted soldier, one of many sent over by the US at the end of World War I.

Henry senior was the son of a German, Leonard Bukowski, who had emigrated to America at the end of the 19th century. There, in Cleveland, he married another German immigrant, Emilie Krause. They set up home in Pasadena and had six children. So, unlike many other American soldiers, Henry Bukowski did not consider Germany to be hell. It was his fatherland. Through one of her brothers, Henry met Katherine Fett, who worked in a bar. He was very tall, she very short. Katherine became his second wife and they lived in Germany until their only son, Charles, was two years old. They moved to the US and, in 1925, settled in Los Angeles.

Bukowski's failure to adapt socially stemmed from his own early life. When he tried to make friends with other children on the east side of Los Angeles where he lived, he found it difficult to fit in: he was shy, his upbringing was not that of the typical American middle classes and he was ridiculed because he had a slight German accent.

When she arrived in America, Bukowski's mother knew hardly any English. Hers was the traditional role in the patriarchal family; she had a master-slave relationship with her husband.

'I always got the idea that she wanted to be on my side but it was an entirely false idea gathered from sucking her nipples at one time.'

And the Bukowskis were so old-fashioned. Perhaps lacking confidence in their own social standing, they were determined to maintain impeccably high standards, making, from the young boy's point of view, unreasonable demands.

In the Depression following the Wall Street Crash of 1929, Charles found himself growing up in a family ruled by the iron hand of an intolerant father who was also not averse to inflicting corporal punishment for the slightest perceived infringement.

As a child, Bukowski was ugly, gloomy and reserved. His complex nature would often make him resort to sarcasm. He felt like a prisoner at home and an outsider at school. The rebelliousness that would inform his entire life was developing inside him.

'I had some pretty terrible parents, and your parents are pretty much your world. That's all there is.'

Henry Bukowski believed in the American dream. He was efficient at work and he had married the woman that God had sent him. He had a house with a garden that was fruitful. He rested on Sunday and abstained from alcohol. He paid his taxes. He was proud to have been a soldier. In public he played the good citizen.

Charles Bukowski (he eventually dropped his first name, Henry) spent half a century doing exactly the opposite. When he could find work, he was the worst possible kind of employee. He set up home with several women and split up with all of them. Only at the end of his life did he own a house with a garden. He drank gallons of alcohol. He avoided paying taxes. He made plain his dislike of 'good' citizens. Although, during World War II, many of his acquaintances enlisted, Bukowski never wore uniform.

As a child, Bukowski suffered from severe acne which would scar him forever; 'I felt as if no woman would ever want to be with me. I saw myself as some kind of freak...'

But the young Bukowski found that when he started drinking alcohol, the pain that had marked his life disappeared for the first time. Also, alcohol would lead to independence. Emboldened by drink, he stood up to his father who merely banished him to sleep in the garage when he smelled alcohol on his breath. And then one day, when he was 19, Hank knocked his father out with a single punch and ran away from home. He would return a few times, but only for brief periods.

In some ways, the psychological experiences of Bukowski's youth seemed to parallel the harsh reality of the time, when the entire country agonized over its destiny, when everyone was hoping for a better tomorrow. He described the breeding ground for his personality in 'Waiting':

...hot summers in the mid-30's Los Angeles, nothing to do, nowhere to go, listening to the terrified talk of our parents at night:
'what will we do? what will we do?'

'god, I don't know...'

Hank (as he was known to his friends) felt himself in fierce conflict with the world. He believed that his parents loved the prestige of having a college student for a son, but showed no interest in his academic studies. On the street, it became clear that the only way he could command respect from his peers was by standing up for himself.

'I don't know how this works, you have to experience it to understand it, but after two people beat on each other eight or nine hours a strange kind of brotherhood emerges.'

In his seventies, Hank would write his memoirs, *Son of Satan*, published in 1990. There he portrayed himself at age 11, as the leader of a gang that had to turn to crime in order to survive: they smoked, got into fights, and even tried to hang a neighbour as a silly practical joke. The account ends with Hank challenging his father to a duel, in which, according to him, he received a brutal punch, straight in the face. He ended up hiding under the bed, cursing his father.

The narrative concludes with this image:

I could hear my father breathing and I moved myself exactly under the center to the head and waited for the next thing.

One might imagine that a terrible beating would ensue, but the writer preferred to leave the story open-ended. So, we see Hank in those days as a boy abused by an adult, resigned to the batterings of fate, but not inclined to expect any mercy. And he was prepared to fight back, if necessary.

2 Poetics and the Bleeding Life

When Hank was in the fifth grade, US President Herbert Hoover was due to attend a ceremony at the Coliseum in Exposition Park, Los Angeles.

Three days later ...

But Bukowski had not even been to the ceremony in the Park. He had simply invented the precisely-detailed story, as he later admitted to his teacher. She was even more impressed. Bukowski had found his vocation. But some time would pass before he could realise his ambition.

In 1932, at the start of Franklin D. Roosevelt's first term as President, Hank was entering high school. However, his real studies would be conducted in his local public library. There, he read Sinclair Lewis, Ernest Hemingway, William Saroyan, Carson McCullers and a little-known writer, John Fante. Those were the writers who most influenced Bukowski's early apprenticeship. Then, in a disordered way, he went on to dip into a host of other writers: ancient Chinese poets, Rabelais, Maupassant, Gorky, Turgenev, Gogol, Tolstoy, Dreiser, Ezra Pound, Shakespeare, Dos Passos, F. Scott Fitzgerald, Aldous Huxley, D. H. Lawrence, e. e. cummings, Conrad, Schopenhauer, Steinbeck, Kant, Hegel, Nietzsche. Bukowski never felt more alone than when reading after dark in that old brownstone building, and never more comforted.

The image of a trapped creature...

Consummation of Grief

I even hear the mountains
the way they laugh
up and down their blue sides
and down in the water
the fish cry
and all the water
is their tears.
I listen to the water
on nights I drink away
and the sadness becomes so great
I hear it in my clock
it becomes knobs upon my dresser
it becomes paper on the floor
it becomes a shoehorn
a laundry ticket

it becomes
cigarette smoke
climbing a chapel of dark vines...
it matters little

very little love is not so bad
or very little life

what counts
is waiting on walls
I was born for this

I was born to hustle roses down the avenues of the dead.

Essential to an understanding
of Bukowski's literary
personality is an appreciation of
his anarchic training at the
public library. On the one hand,
nothing of the academic
approach rubbed off on him
Indeed, his style would seem to
defy literary logic—his
punctuation, for instance,
ignored basic grammatical rules.
On the other hand, his voracious
and compulsive reading—almost
a fundamental need for
survival—would give him a
poetic sensitivity which was
direct, without affectation, and
unique to him.

In the poem 'The Burning of the Dream', written after a fire had destroyed the library where he had discovered the world of literature, Hank acknowledges his debt:

**it is
thanks
to my luck
and my way
that this library was
there when I was
young and looking to
hold on to
something
when there seemed very
little about.**

It was as if Hank was living his life through those books in the library; escaping from the violence and mundanity of his daily life, making friends with the characters and writers he encountered. In an article entitled 'A Rambling Essay on Poetics and the Bleeding Life Written while Drinking a Six-Pack (Tall)', published in 1965, Hank describes his view of those days:

'When I was becoming a genius, when I was dying of hunger, and nobody wanted to publish me, I spent even more time in the library than I have ever since. It was wonderful to get a seat by a window in the sunlight where the sun could fill my head with music.'

I turned against my friends. Almost all of them came from families wealthier than mine. They had an easy life. I knew that such a life couldn't be mine.

1939

Charles

On graduation night Charles was hiding outside the school gym, ashamed of the scars that the acne had left. He could only peek at the dance through a window. He felt embarrassed, especially about being intellectually opposed to the festivities. And he felt envious of the crowd. He would have given anything to be one of them, if only he could have been less of a rebel.

That night, a janitor threw Bukowski
out of the building,
mistaking him for an intruder.

The next day, Charles had a pivotal conversation with his parents. His father derided his wish to become a writer and they had an argument in which both parents seemed united against him. His mother cried. From that moment, Charles decided that, as soon as possible, he had to get on with the rest of his life. His priorities were:

3 Running in the Cage

In order to escape the parental home, Hank accepted the first job he found which was with the Sears Roebuck department store on Olympic Boulevard in LA.

So began Bukowski's experiences as a wage slave.

'This would be one of my first lessons. They expected people to give their entire lives, and all their loyalty, to some shit job.'

But the employers were not the only ones to blame:
'...don't kid yourself—many people want SLAVERY, a job, 2 jobs, anything to keep them running in the cage.'

The young would-be writer had little respect for his workmates, who were of his parents' generation. In 1982, he would describe them in the novel *Ham on Rye*:

Four men and three women. They were all old. They seemed to have salivary problems. Little clumps of spittle had formed at the corners of their mouths; the spittle had dried and turned white and then been coated by new wet spittle. Some of them were too thin, others too fat. Some were near-sighted; others trembled. One old fellow in a brightly colored shirt had a hump on his back. They all smiled and coughed, puffing at cigarettes.

He did not last long in his first job. However, he had, in 1940, enrolled at Los Angeles University. At City College on Western Avenue, his gaunt appearance caused a stir and his air of superiority did not go down well. But Bukowski created a distinct impression.

He signed up for several courses including journalism, dramatic art, English and history. He felt it would not be a bad idea to earn his living as a journalist. In the end, it was all writing. But it would be twenty years before he would write regularly for a daily newspaper.

At the time, the university was full of left-wing militants, but politics were not important to Hank. Naturally, he set himself against the general tide of student thinking.

Yet on another occasion...

'I used to lean slightly toward the liberal left but the crew that's involved, in spite of the ideas, are a thin & grafted-like type of human, blank-eyed and throwing words like vomit. essentially they are very lonely. the secret is really that they have not put society down but that society has put them down and so now they gather and hand-hold through 1/4 souls and play at tinkertoy games with 1/8 minds. there's nothing left to do except admit that they are slugs, worms, and they are not going to do that.'

Despite continuing battles with his father, and an inhospitable home life, Bukowski had found some solace: he was writing short stories. Although he felt that he needed to embark on the course the rest of his life would take, he was anaesthetised by the relative physical comfort of his home life. He was not happy, but he had grown accustomed to it.

Ironically, it was Hank's early attempts at writing that would forcibly launch him into his new life. His father had found some of Hank's manuscripts in a desk drawer and was so disgusted by what he read that he threw the papers and the typewriter out of the window.

His mother told Hank what had happened. He went back to the house and, shouting from the street, challenged his father to a fight. Henry senior stayed indoors. Hank knew that the time had come to leave.

Charles moved to down-
town LA. In a hotel full of
Filipino immigrants, he
found a room for $1.50 a
week. Each day he found
out more about what life as
an adult would be.

Now that he was free at last from any parental control, and with
all the writing in the world ahead of him, the country itself suddenly
stood on a precipice. The threat of another war was all over the
newspapers, but Hank was not willing to subscribe blindly to the tide
of patriotism:

**'It wasn't long before all the tall blond boys had
formed The Abraham Lincoln Brigade—to hold
off the hordes of fascism in Spain. And then had
their asses shot off by trained troops. Some of them
did it for adventure and a trip to Spain but they
still got their asses shot off. I liked my ass.'**

From now on, for the next thirty years, until the publication of *Post Office*, Bukowski would choose to escape from the mainstream, hiding on the dark side of the American dream.

In fact, most of his literary output hinges on the adventures and misadventures of his descent into hell—the hell of being poor in a society that only values the ability to make money.

Although critics would compare his writing to that of Ernest Hemingway and others, Bukowski saw fundamental differences:

[Hemingway] wrote about major themes—freedom, patriotism, courage, the power of the will, destiny. I write about people who don't earn enough to pay the rent, about women dying in public hospitals, about children abandoned by their parents.

They'll compare me to the Beat Generation: Kerouac, Allen Ginsberg, William Burroughs, Gregory Corso. But they were very different. They preferred jazz while I prefer classical music. Drugs fascinated them, I drink cheap beer. They played with politics, I play the horses.

In 1942 there began a period of travelling, through New Orleans, Atlanta, Fort Worth, Sacramento, Philadelphia, St Louis, San Francisco and New York, moving from job to job, fight to fight, woman to woman and one drunken binge to another

During those first years of his adult life, Bukowski cultivated a rather romantic image of himself. He felt that one day the world would come to know of his suffering. So he would accept the sacrifice; a life of deprivation was a necessary part of the story of his life. He was like a boxer in training for the toughest of fights.

Through those hard times, Hank kept on writing, in miserable guest houses and hotels. He sent his writings to magazines and reviews throughout the country. He gambled what little money he won at the races. He liked the minimalist lifestyle, having no greater dream than literary glory.

He felt like a member of the underground before the underground movement even existed. He was one of life's deviants, eccentrics, dissidents—a refugee and fugitive from Parnassus, at a time when nobody knew that any 'counterculture' was possible.

He was a tough character who lived from day to day, thinking only of getting enough money for his next drink and cheap meal. When he pawned his typewriter, he wrote in notebooks and jotters. But he did not get depressed; his cure was to go to the races, and he got over it.

If, when he left home, he saw himself as the hero of an action adventure, the young writer gradually realised that, in order to earn a little money, the only possible adventure was survival:

'...fun and danger hardly put margarine on toast or fed the cat. You give up toast and end up eating the cat.'

Flophouse

you haven't lived
until you've been in a
flophouse
with nothing but one
light bulb
and 56 men
squeezed together
on cots
with everybody
snoring
at once
and some of those
snores
so
deep and
gross and
unbelievable—
dark
snotty
gross
subhuman
wheezings
from hell
itself...

Bukowski details the degrada-
tion, squalor and despair of
the hopeless inhabitants of the
flophouse, acknowledging his
own descent into hell.

Meanwhile, thousands of young men, filled with patriotism, were being drafted into the army. But Bukowski had, unintentionally, managed to elude the government while roaming from city to city. He was arrested in Philadelphia and spent a night in jail. However, he was declared insane by a military psychiatrist. The doctor had in his files some papers that the FBI had seized from the hotel room where Bukowski was arrested. A line from one of them read:

4 Don't Know Who I Am

Hank had been writing copiously, and collecting numerous rejections. His first published essay, in *Story* magazine, had reflected the situation. It was called

AFTERMATH OF A LENGTHY REJECTION SLIP by BUKOWSKI

Story magazine was edited by Whit Burnett, whom Bukowski admired because he had taken the trouble to explain why he had rejected all the earlier efforts. Burnett paid him $25 which, at that time, was a small fortune for Bukowski. Yet seeing himself in print produced a strange reaction, which was almost inexplicable considering the enthusiasm with which he had embarked on his chosen career.

The young writer became deeply depressed. He had persuaded himself that either the publishers were doing him a favour, or it was simply his perseverance that had finally won them over. Bukowski had ceased to be the impulsive, optimistic young man. He often thought of suicide. As a result, Bukowski says, he gave up writing—the thing that mattered most to him—for the next ten years:

I'm not good, just persistent.

'I packed it in. I threw away all the stories and concentrated upon drinking. I didn't feel that the publishers were ready and that although I was ready, I could be readier...'

He may well have given up writing consistently, but during that period, a number of short stories were published.

Working on the theory that people wanted 'beautiful lies', he had not yet discovered that his own life was of literary interest. Caresse Crosby, the publisher of the review *Portfolio*, was amazed at the quality and style of a Bukowski piece called 'Twenty Tanks from Kasseldown', which she wanted to publish. She wrote to him, asking 'Who are you?' Bukowski, reflecting his self-doubt, replied:

Dear Mrs. Crosby
I don't know who I am.
Sincerely yours,
—Charles Bukowski

A major contributory factor in Bukowski's reluctance to write was his relationship with Jane Cooney Baker.

Let's say that I didn't give up writing for nothing.

I gave it up to have time to get drunk.

Jane Cooney Baker was ten years older than Bukowski. She had diligently devoted herself to becoming an alcoholic in an attempt to overcome a personal tragedy: her husband, from whom she was separated, but whom she still loved, had died in a car crash.

The story of Jane and Bukowski played an important part in his later work. It inspired much of the script for the film *Barfly*, which Barbet Schroeder was to direct in 1987. Jane appeared under different names and guises in many of Bukowski's writings. Apart from his last wife, she was the woman who had the greatest immediate influence on him.

If in previous years the writer had condemned himself to economic and social hardship, in this long, ill-fated period he descended into his own personal hell: that of alcoholism with its consequent health problems.

Hank's relationship with Jane was tempestuous and it was peppered with violent fights and his affairs with other women. During one of the inevitable stormy periods, he wrote a poem which reflected the sordid world in which he was living, and the humour he used to deal with his own personal torture.

The poem, detailing his fantasy of a willing, compliant 'whore', is written with a directness and honesty that sets the author apart from most other writers:

A Man's Woman

the dream of a man
is a whore with a gold tooth...

... who will stay a week
just one week,
and wash the dishes and cook and fuck and suck
and scrub the kitchen floor...

...just stay one week
just one week
and do the thing and go and never come
back
for that one earring on the dresser.

Bukowski's attitude to women was somewhat ambivalent. He seemed at once fascinated by and repelled by them, dismissive of them. He described women as 'bitches', 'whores', and sex was often violent, rarely tender. Bukowski even wrote and spoke of his fantasies of sex with little girls. Having come to sex relatively late in life (he had his first sexual experience when he was 23), he seemed at once sexually obsessed and naive. He veered between objectifying women and idolising them, between distrust and awe.

And yet, Bukowski did feel real compassion, almost paternal in its nature, for that tragic woman, Jane. When her final hours drew near in 1962, she did get in touch with him even though they had been physically separated for some time.

Mortified and at times repentant, Hank took stock of the situation. He was more than anxious about the precariousness of Jane's life, which seemed to him to stem from emotions deep inside her being. He was at her bedside in the hospital when she died and he paid for her modest funeral. Prostrated by her death, he wrote a poem for her, curiously entitled 'Uruguay or Hell', describing his feelings as he stands by her graveside:

Uruguay or Hell

**...and so there I was
standing there—
durable
visible
clothed
waiting....**

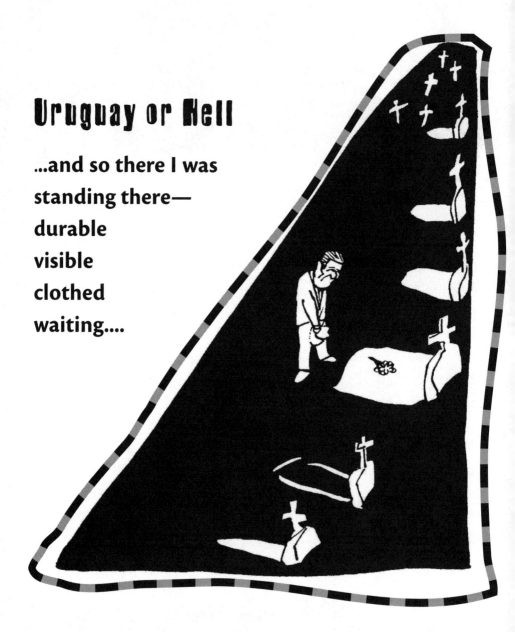

and while the Catholic pries argues over the 'technicalities' of the burial and the woman's son worries about the cost:

...I was the lover and I cared but what I cared for was dead.

In 1952, Bukowski had got the only more or less stable job he ever had: he joined the LA post office, at a time when many new temporary employees were being taken on.

It all begins and ends with the mailbox, and when they find a way to remove mailboxes, much of our suffering will end.

Thus began his stint as a postman, which would last three years. His alcohol-related problems meant that another three years would be spent trudging between work and hospitals until 1958 when a twelve-year period began as a sorting-office clerk, which ended with his resignation in 1969.

In those dark years as a postman, Hank had to earn enough to support both himself and Jane. Most of the time, she was not working and spent her life waiting for Hank to come home, drinking endlessly and going to the race-track. It was life on a collision course. But at the same time Bukowski's life experiences, later to explode into his writing, constituted a kind of chronicle of self-destruction that few writers would be able to emulate.

In 1956, Hank woke up in the emergency room following one of his drinking bouts. He was coughing up blood. He had a bleeding stomach ulcer and was close to death. His life was saved by a blood transfusion—arranged by his father.

When he was discharged from the hospital, a nurse prescribed a strict diet. One doctor suggested surgery, another gave a serious warning:

'Drinking is only to jell the parts that have been taken apart by factories or whores or a faceful of busses. I mean, that it brings me back to the basics of myself, whatever those basics may be. If drinking destroys the brain, fine. For what my brain has seen it yearns destruction.'

But his stay in hospital had a positive effect within a few months: thinking that his days were numbered, Bukowski started to write again. And, almost exclusively, poetry.

It was like a kind of madness. I didn't even think about what I was going to write. It was completely automatic.

Literature was his therapy for the ulcer. But he did not give up drinking. Even though he dedicated a large part of each day to writing —'discipline' became another addiction— Bukowski did not revert to the fantasies of his youth, those 'beautiful lies'. He simply created literature out of what had happened, what was happening all around him. In those ten years when he had thrown himself into living (badly) he had matured as a writer.

In 1986, turning his back on polemics, he would publish a humorous poem which shows his way of dealing with reality. Writing with the toughness and dexterity of a boxer jabbing at his opponent's chin, he chronicles his parents' dismissal of his desire to be a writer, ending with typical sardonic self-deprecation:

they were my earliest literary critics and they both were right.

'dear pa and ma'

In his forties, Hank felt like a survivor. He could see his work as the intimate journal of somebody who had miraculously cheated death many times. He no longer had the optimism of the fledgling writer. But he had not lost his good humour. So, he was rather like...

An Optimistic Pessimist.

JESUS CHI
SAVES FROM
ALL SIN. PRAY
TO JESUS NOW.
OBEY THE BIBLE

TAKE
ONE
PAPER
FREE

WARNING:
DEATH.
JUDGMENT
ETERNITY,
HEAVEN or HELL

His poems began to be published in underground reviews all over the country. He was forging a literary reputation for himself that made him feel that life was beginning to make sense. He no longer dreamed of being famous. He revelled in the knowledge that what he was writing was truly interesting. However, his financial problems were not over. After a break caused by illness, he was once again caught in 'the horror of the post office'.

While pursuing outlets for his writing, Hank had proposed by mail to an editor with whom he had been corresponding, but whom he had never met. He married Barbara Frye in October 1955, but they were completely unsuited and divorced two years later.

In 1957, Hank's mother died suddenly. Before her death, she confessed to him: 'You were right, Henry. Your father is a horrible man'.

The Twins

In 1959, when his father died, Bukowski described their relationship in his poem 'The Twins', showing the remorse of a survivor.

**I move through my father's house (on which he owed
$8,000 after 20 years
on the same job) and look at his dead shoes
the way his feet curled the leather as if he was angrily plant-
ing roses,
and he was...**

> **...to die on a kitchen floor at 7 o'clock in the morning
> while other people are frying eggs
> is not so rough
> unless it happens to you....**

Hank inherited his parents' house. But he got rid of it. He sold it, paid off the mortgage and in a few days wasted the profit on drink, women and horseracing. It was as if that money—which could have helped him straighten out his wayward life—was burning his hands, or as if he was trying to exorcise childhood memories.

5 Blood on the Line

In 1960, E.V. Griffith, the editor of the review *Hearse* decided to publish Bukowski's collected poems. His very first book, *Flower, Fist and Bestial Wail*, was 14 pages long. He received his advance copies on his 40th birthday and celebrated all on his own, drinking first in a strip joint and then bar-hopping.

'For me to get paid for writing is like going to bed with a beautiful woman and afterwards she gets up, goes to her purse and gives me a handful of money. I'll take it.'

The new decade was to be a turbulent one. Most writers made political compromises, adopting ideas and attitudes which appealed to college students. Bukowski considered them demagogues.

If I hear on the radio 40 orphans died in a fire in Vermont, how can I feel it?

It's just information coming over a dead wire.

So, what about the anti-war protests?

I warned about people who scream for peace. They are the ones who will murder you in the end.

Nothing could have been more alien to Hank than the world of social compromise or politics. Those things seemed to him—and it was not a pose, rather, one of life's truths—to be at the very core of everything he was opposed to.

58

Politicians seemed to be looking for ways to tap into the public mood. Bukowski's poem 'Face of a Political Candidate on a Street Billboard' clearly contrasted his own life with that of people who hoped to win votes.

**there he is
not too many hangovers
not too many fights with women
not too many flat tires
never thought of suicide...**

...he'll be elected.

Bukowski remained disillusioned and sceptical about politics:

'Before you kill something make sure you have something better to replace it with; something better than political opportunist slamming hate horseshit in the public park...I have no politics, I observe.'

In stark contrast to what had happened 15 years before with his first short stories, the publication of his 14-page book was a creative leap forward for Hank. In fact, in the sixties, despite having to go on working for the post office, he produced 14 books, not to mention his collaborations with underground magazines of all kinds. Hank became a kind of guru for many American underground writers.

Now that he was emerging from the cloistered existence of the drunkard who shuts himself in a room in order to write feverishly, as if possessed, hundreds of would-be writers, rebelling against official culture, saw Bukowski as a kind of movie star. Except that Bukowski was within reach.

Bukowski's number was in the phone book. He received dozens of calls every day from all kinds of fans who, when they got through, were his only contact with the outside world.

In some ways, that is when he began to really write—as would become clearer after *Post Office*. He travelled back through his life, in a sense looking for explanations.

Confessions of a Man Insane Enough to Live with Beasts (1965) and *All the Assholes in the World and Mine* (1966) show a return to the abandoned style of prose of his mid-forties.

Critics would see those years as a kind of incubation period for what was to come. Both those pieces were autobiographical, written almost automatically, as fast as he could type, with no revision or elaboration.

I have nothing to invent. I have lived and I want to put that in writing.

Bukowski made almost a cult out of writing just as he spoke. He loathed the kind of literature in which high-flown words were used; it seemed to him abstract, so foreign to the vocabulary of the people he himself knew.

Writing has to be blood on the line.

Hemingway was interesting when he was young.

Henry Miller was worthwhile, obsessed with sex.

So it's only possible to write when you are young or pretending to be...

'A good style comes primarily from a lack of pretentiousness, and what is pretentious changes from year to year from day to day from minute to minute. We must be ever more careful. A man does not get old because he nears death; a man gets old because he can no longer see the false from the good.'

The third book of prose published in the sixties, *Notes of a Dirty Old Man*, was a collection of articles that had appeared in *Open City*, an underground Los Angeles newspaper. Hank was by then a recognised writer in California.

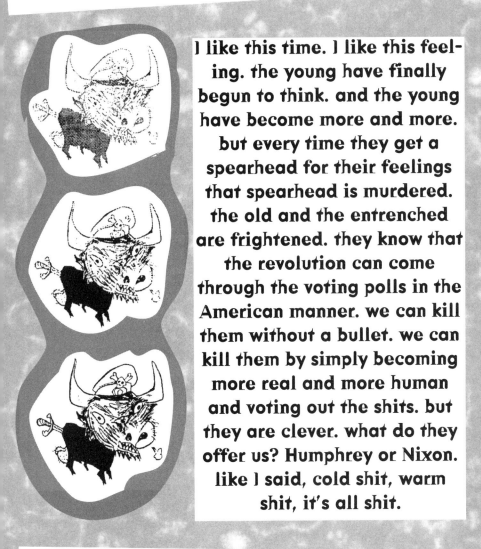

I like this time. I like this feeling. the young have finally begun to think. and the young have become more and more. but every time they get a spearhead for their feelings that spearhead is murdered. the old and the entrenched are frightened. they know that the revolution can come through the voting polls in the American manner. we can kill them without a bullet. we can kill them by simply becoming more real and more human and voting out the shits. but they are clever. what do they offer us? Humphrey or Nixon. like I said, cold shit, warm shit, it's all shit.

His newspaper column had, however, brought problems at work. The post office bureaucrats took a dim view of an employee who told thousands of readers about his adventures on the fringe. Nevertheless, these writings gave him the opportunity to see his controversial, polemical views in print—and accepted as normal.

In life, Hank experimented with sin and bad behaviour, challenging correctness. In his writings, he developed his own style of punctuation, which was contrived and artificial. He described himself as a sexual victim and he mixed poetry and obscenity as if he were an alchomist, performing daring, new experiments.

...yet, I still have a little distance and after 2,000 pieces of ass, most of them not very good, I am still able to laugh at myself and my trap.

'Notes of a Dirty Old Man'

The women who cry over you and screw you, they'll all abandon you, send you birthday cards and won't let you have the peace to forget the desolation, the terror, the anguish, the failure all of life's ups and downs with their sly winks and tears.

When he saw that his opinions went beyond the literary milieu, he was delighted to have found such a huge pulpit. One of his first articles for *Open City*, for example, was a critique of a biography of Hemingway. Entitled 'An Old Drunk Who Ran out of Luck', it ended with the judgement:

Through his opinions on literature, which contradicted established views, *Notes of a Dirty Old Man* shows much of Hank's own personality, combining caustic humour—most often directed at himself—with an almost limitless existential despair. The narcissistic writer, sometimes using the pseudonym 'Stirkoff', wrote opinions such as:

'Burroughs is a very dull writer;...outside of Dreiser, Thomas Wolfe is the worst American writer ever born;...Faulkner is nothing except to very dry Southern extremists...'

His bosses at the post office were putting pressure on him They were jealous of the notoriety that a lowly employee was gaining. Asked to give a psychological assessment of Bukowski, one of his superiors commented:

Notes of a Dirty Old Man was an almost instant success. It was Bukowski's first such experience. Twenty thousand copies were sold within a few months. It was an incredible example of word-of-mouth publicity, which would introduce many more people to the new cult of that extraordinary personality, Bukowski, a virtual icon of iconoclasts. Soon the book appeared in Germany, the first European country to 'discover' this exceptional new writer. After all, he was in a sense one of their own. One of the articles in the book is a collection of aphorisms with the stamp of Bukowski all over them. He declared that they were written 'scribbling on shirt cardboard during two day drunks'.

Beautiful thoughts, and beautiful women never last

if you want to know where God is, ask a drunk.

the difference between Art and Life is that Art
is more bearable

The well balanced individual is insane

Almost everybody is born a genius and buried an idiot

an intellectual is a man who says a simple thing in
a difficult way; an artist is a man who says a difficult
thing in a simple way.

if you want to know who your friends are, get
yourself a jail sentence.

During that decade when he tried to lead some kind of regular life, Hank fathered his only child, Marina. She was born of a relationship with Frances Smith, one of several admirers with whom Bukowski had more or less casual affairs. Frances, like Jane, was a confident, mature woman. She already had four children when she met Hank in 1962.

She knew that she and he would never make a perfect couple. She knew too that the ideal marriage would not be possible with Hank.

In 1963, when she was pregnant, Frances dropped the idea of getting married and instead proposed an open relationship. Marina Bukowski was born on 7 September 1964, while her father was reading Plato in the waiting room outside the maternity ward at a public hospital.

Hank wanted to be a good father, but that was impossible while he was leading the lifestyle he had chosen. It was difficult to divide his time between his family, work and the demands of his growing literary status. Frances and Hank gradually drifted apart, but she would always have a place in his affections. And Hank maintained a very special relationship with Marina, right up to the time of his death. Yet he rarely wrote about her.

In 1969, when economic hardship was about to become a thing of the past, Bukowski's friends persuaded him to consider giving a poetry reading. It may be hard to believe, but he was shy and inarticulate in front of strangers. He gave his first reading in a Los Angeles gallery and it turned out to be a success, with over 300 people in the audience.

He repeated the performance the following day. When he realised that this could be a source of considerable extra income—he could earn in a single day what a postal worker could earn in a whole year—it at last dawned on him that the time had come for him to free himself from regular work. He resigned from the post office.

Los Angeles
3 January 1970

Bukowski was 49 when he began his first novel. He had spent 12 years working Monday to Friday in a sorting office, a place that he detested. Altogether, eighteen years had passed since he had joined the postal service, working first as a postman, delivering letters in some of the toughest districts of Los Angeles.

In the remaining 24 years of his life, Bukowski would publish 45 books in succession, almost without a break.

6 Post Office

On 21 January 1970, after 18 days in a kind of trance, during which he had written 120,000 words—which he cut to 90,000—the work of producing his first, and most famous, novel was complete. Bukowski called his publisher, John Martin:

Like almost all of Bukowski's work, *Post Office*, is autobiographical, the protagonist, Henry Chinaski, being his alter ego. Chinaski is, above all, a fearless man who is at the same time a loser. He is a cynic with a sense of humour, but he is also vulnerable; a sensitive man hardened by society.

Those people at the post office thought they were doing me a favour by giving me a job.

But I was the one doing them a favour. I gave them so many years of my life doing work that stopped me writing.

Post Office, published in January 1971, settled old scores with the alienating world of work. The novel opens 'It began as a mistake...' From then on, the reader is drawn into a succession of scenes that portray the comedy of the human condition: when you hate work, it can be like a life sentence; love can be like a double-edged sword; those without money have to resign themselves to having none, while those with power can only use it arbitrarily. Solutions to one's problems, says Chinaski/ Bukowski, can be only be found when you take hold of the reins of your own life.

It would be half a century before Hank managed to 'take hold of the reins' of his own life. To him, this achievement represented a triumph of the individual over the masses; it was the victory of individual will over the social order.

On this subject he wrote:

Beware
The Average Man
The Average Woman
BEWARE Their Love
Their Love Is Average, Seeks
Average
But There Is Genius In Their Hatred
There is Enough Genius In Their
Hatred To Kill You, To Kill
Anybody...

...They Will Attempt To Destroy
Anything
That Differs
From Their Own

   Not Being Able
   To Create Art
   They Will Not
   Understand Art

The Genius of the Crowd

The most serious accusation that Bukowski could throw at society in his work was that it intimidates people by means of a complex system of control—institutions—condemning them to accepting humiliation and failure as the norm. According to Bukowski, those who do not rebel lose the ability to think for themselves. They are the 'common people'. As for the rest, they may well fare no better. Bukowski expressed his world view in the poem 'footnote upon the construction of the masses': those who are different will be 'eliminated'...

by the police, by their mothers, their brothers, others; by themselves.

With the publication of *Post Office*, Bukowski began to gain greater recognition as a writer. He realised that he need no longer feel ashamed to face the landlords, to whom for many long, hard years he had had to pay $37.50 a month in rent. Having eked that out of his income, he still needed to find money to:

1. Buy alcohol
2. Bet on horses
3 Pay child support for his daughter
4. Get just enough food to stay alive

From then on, Hank became ever more famous, more and more wealthy. And, as a writer, more and more prolific. This came as a relief to those who had been aware of Bukowski's past suffering. Yet it disappointed many of his admirers, who were enthralled by the old myth of the artist dying of hunger.

In fact, before *Post Office*, Bukowski was already a reputable underground poet with a widespread cult following throughout America. Even so, he was not yet truly famous—at least not as famous as he was about to become.

Earning a living was a continuous, necessary chore, until *Post Office* came out. There have been few writers so marginalised, so alienated from the cultural stereotypes, so entwined with those on the losing end of capitalism.

A STAR IS BORN

With the *Dirty Old Man* collection having achieved cult status, the publication of *Post Office* in 1971, was a huge success, with over 40,000 copies sold. From then on, Bukowski never had any major financial problems—and young, attractive women started to pass through his life.

Linda King, a writer and sculptress, and Liza Williams, a record producer, were his most regular companions in the early seventies.

Sex is interesting, but it's not totally important. I mean its not even as important (physically) as excretion. A man can go seventy years without a piece of ass, but he can die in a week without a bowel movement.

As a celebrity writer, he began to attract media attention. Part of the Bukowski legend—the accursed writer in an accursed city—was promoted by a TV special produced by the young director Taylor Hackford. Working for the LA channel KCET, Hackford made a documentary on Bukowski's life, moving constantly between public and private episodes from a turbulent period of his life. Television is, obviously, like a huge magnifying glass and it certainly magnified Hank's personality.

'Bukowski', was transmitted on 25 November 1973. Despite the complaints from viewers who felt that a writer who constantly used the word 'fuck' was unacceptable on TV, the programme was an enormous hit. It won the Los Angeles Corporation for Public Broadcasting award for best cultural programme of the year, and soon after, it was shown at the influential Museum of Modern Art in New York.

Hackford included a poetry reading that Hank had given in San Francisco. It took place after some conscientious drinking to overcome an attack of nerves. The cameras caught him throwing up and abusing the audience, who shouted back. Faced with the ensuing mayhem, Bukowski behaved like a rock star, high on his own adrenaline. However, as soon as he started to read, the waters were calmed and the reading ended amid applause.

After that, Bukowski was shown smoking a joint and
drinking more alcohol. He was much more interested in being
seen as the ultimate sinner, than merely as somebody under
the effect of dope. Years later, in more tolerant times, when his
prestige was beyond dispute, there appeared in his writings
some mention of LSD and cocaine, nearly always used and/or
offered by his 'freaky' friends.

It seemed that the rules of the punk movement, which in the mid
seventies had eclipsed earlier concepts of rock music, had translated
to the world of literature.

Bukowski's performance style was indeed bizarre: he would begin by behaving boorishly, but when the time came for him to read, he oscillated between abusing and charming his audiences.

'I hate precious poets and I hate precious audiences too.'

'if the world digs me it is only to bury me.'

7 A Duel to the Death

The title of his next book heightened his risqué image. It was a book of short stories called *Erections, Ejaculations and General Tales of Ordinary Madness* (1972). Hank saw this book as fodder for the monster book trade, giving him time to write his second novel *Factotum*. Before that came out, he published another book of short stories, *South of No North* (1973), which must have given the impression that, far from being a conventional writer, Bukowski was an assembly line. Most readers were unaware that his productivity stemmed from the autobiographical nature of his work and that this kind of writing was a form of therapy.

His method was simple: he got over his past by making it public. And he got paid for it! In the seventies he published ten books, one a year on average.

It's like this. I threw myself into living and now that's what I'm writing about. If I'd wanted to be happy, I'd have played tennis.

In 'Guts', one of the best stories in *South of No North*, Hank described himself:

Like anybody can tell you, I am not a very nice man. I don't know the word. I have always admired the villain, the outlaw, the son of a bitch. I don't like the clean-shaven boy with the necktie and the good job. I like desperate men, men with broken teeth and broken minds and broken ways... I'm more interested in perverts than saints. I can relax with bums because I am a bum. I don't like laws, morals, religions, rules. I don't like to be shaped by society.

Hank found the title of *Factotum* while looking up a word in the dictionary. The novel resulted from a desire to paint a definitive picture of his life in the forties. He began work on it in 1973. It took him two years to complete.

That journey into the time when living in the depths of poverty was nothing compared to living with his parents, made Hank see himself with the compassion of the adult he had for so long refused to become.

**Frankly I was horrified by life, at
what a man had to do simply in
order to eat, sleep, and keep himself
clothed. So I stayed in bed and
drank. When you drank the world was
still out there, but for the moment it
didn't have you by the throat.**

In 1982, Fernanda Pivano, a literary critic, published a book that included a transcript of a three-hour interview with Bukowski. *What I Like Best Is Scratching My Pits* marked *Factotum* as the beginning of Bukowski's maturity: according to Pivano, it gave a better account of the author's development than his previous stories had done, and it abandoned the ingenuousness of his early works.

The protagonist of Factotum does not struggle against the inanity of the universe but confines himself to demonstrating the lack of direction in the lives of the masses; lives alienated by depersonalization, chained to economic necessity, paralysed by the impossibility of freedom from the brief journey along the short road that leads to the grave.

Such were the themes of the non-violent protests of the fifties and sixties in North America. Bukowski approached those social issues in an altogether different manner from the principal players in the arena of public dissent. His approach was indeed that of the proletariat or sub-proletariat even, but also that of an aspiring poet, an aspiring writer.

In 1976 Bukowski met Linda Lee Beighle, the woman with whom he would spend the last 18 years of his life. He was 64, she 32. He was the great Bukowski and she was an ex-hippie, vegetarian, owner of a beach restaurant and a devotee of the Indian guru Meher Baba.

Their relationship developed very slowly and culminated in marriage in 1985. Bukowski sold photographs taken during their romance to *Penthouse* magazine.

In spite of all the things that might,
at the beginning, have driven them
apart, including his jealousy and
violence towards Linda, the couple's
relationship underwent a curious symbiosis:
Hank gradually stopped womanizing, started to
pay attention to his physical well-being and
transformed himself into a tolerant husband.

Linda drank heavily, but also became preoccupied
with her health. She never took part in any
decisions about their personal life. Hank wrote to
a friend 'Yes, Linda Lee is a good woman. I was
due for some luck... I've had some bad ones, many
bad ones. The percentages have come around
and I am able to accept them'.

Inspired by his relationship with Linda, Hank finished his third novel, *Women*, in October 1978. It is his longest book — 433 pages divided into 99 chapters. *Women* was partly inspired by Boccaccio's *Decameron*, a book in praise of eroticism.

In it, he focuses on his first years of fame. One critic complained that, as a novel, *Women* lacked structure. Hank agreed.

Love is ridiculous because it can't last.

Women is not about love but about sex. It deals with his relationships with twenty or so women of all kinds. Those encounters occurred after a four-year period of celibacy resulting from the alcoholism that nearly killed him. The book could be seen as a farewell to those crazy years, since he had found the woman of his dreams and his wayward past needed to be buried. In fact, this third volume of his lengthy review of the past begins to dispel the grief that shrouds *Post Office* and *Factotum*. From it emerges a kind of joyousness, though it is sprinkled with irony.

Sex is ridiculous because it doesn't last long enough.

The book begins with a typical complaint:

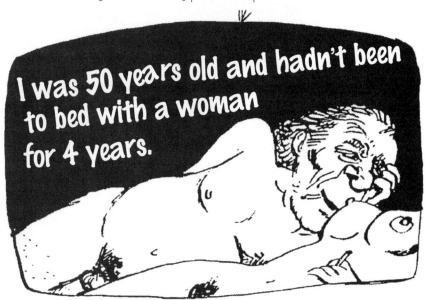

I was 50 years old and hadn't been to bed with a woman for 4 years.

And it ends with his meeting an old cat on his doorstep. The meaning is clear: women may stream through a man's life but in the end he is alone, and must prepare himself for being alone. In one passage, he writes:

Human relationships didn't work anyhow. Only the first two weeks had any zing, then the participants lost their interest. Masks dropped away and real people began to appear... Modern society had created its own kind and they feasted on each other. It was a duel to   the death in a cesspool.

Fernanda Pivano concludes: 'Now Bukowski is writing without insecurity. He writes with unquestionable facility and agility. Clearly that derives from years of experience. He is aware of his place among other important writers, but he continues to display his disapproval of official culture'.

Ah, you are Chinaski, the legendary Chinaski. You have presence, an image that speaks for itself in the students' quarters where you spend the night after one of your readings.

The staff here are reading Truman Capote. I only read the racing results.

I confine myself to being. Apart from that, I intend to remember and to ramble on.

In love with Linda, with whom he frequently went to the races, and maintaining a simple, low-profile lifestyle, he published more than ever before.

His publishers pointed out that it was not a good idea to saturate the market but that did not matter to him. In the middle of 1977 he was producing, on average, twenty poems a week, along with prose narratives.

His book of poems, *Love is a Dog from Hell* (1977), contained much of the groundwork for his fourth novel (*Ham on Rye*); it reviews the extraordinary series of relationships he had had with women of all classes and backgrounds. Bukowski was bidding a public farewell to the dissolute life. Sentimental anarchy was almost at an end. And he was no longer alone, nor would he ever be again.

In 1988 Linda and Hank bought a house at San Pedro, in the north of Los Angeles, close to the sea and to the highways that would take Hank to the racetracks at Santa Anita and Hollywood Park. He was earning so much in royalties that, on the advice of his accountant, he converted that capital into real estate in order to pay less tax. In his fifth novel, *Hollywood*, he recorded that...

There was a huge hedge in front on the street and the yard was also in front so the house sat way back on the lot. It looked like a damned good place to hide.

There was even a stairway, an upstairs with a bedroom, bathroom and what was to become my typing room. And there was an old desk left in there, a huge ugly old thing. Now, after decades, I was a writer with a desk. Yes, I felt the fear, the fear of becoming like them.

This period gave rise to the image of Hank as a hard-hearted, macho man and as a loathsome misogynist. Many readers who were not *au fait* with his life history took the descriptions in *Women* as an indication of his true personality. When the critics took him seriously, he responded in an interview:

I make insulting remarks about myself and about many men and women. But there are women who are stuck with the roles they've chosen for themselves. They are the partisans in the battle of the sexes. They attack me more than anyone else.

Soon after, there was a militant feminist demonstration against him. Hank was annoyed at first but then responded with humour.

I don't want to argue with women who wear moustaches.

It is ironic that those critics attacked him at the very time when he had at last found—as he had prayed for, years before, in a poem—'a decent woman' to whom he could, without embarrassment, say the words 'for always'.

Yes

my average relationship lasts
two and a half years.
with wars
inflation
unemployment
alcoholism
gambling
and my own degenerate nervousness
I think I do well enough....

...there is much good in being alone
but there is a strange warmth in not being alone....

...I like it when there's a knock on the door and
she's there....

Hank would live in the San Pedro house until his death. There he had the privacy he needed and a peace without precedent. He extended his study by putting in a kind of alcove with a skylight, where he wrote at night, while Linda was sleeping.

'There is only one place to write and that is alone at a typewriter. The writer who has to go into the streets is a writer who does not know the streets... when you leave your typewriter you leave your machine gun and the rats come pouring through.'

Hank's old friends were amazed to see him adapting to a clean, ordered house, with all the trappings of the wealthy Los Angeles middle classes. But most of all, their eyes were drawn to the picture of the guru above the door. Had Hank been *converted* as well?

Fear and Madness

barricaded here on the 2nd floor
chair against the door
butcher knife on table
I type my first poem here...

He admits that his life has changed, that he is writing the poem for his accountant and that, reminiscent of his father, he now owns a house, garden and trees. But still, a sense of impending failure invades the poem:

...I can fail in many ways now
I was always good at that....

...barricaded here on the 2nd floor
I am in a small room again.

8 Europe

In May 1978, accompanied by Linda and the photographer Michael Montfort, Hank returned to Germany, 53 years after being taken to America by his parents. In Mannheim, Hank gave his only poetry reading outside the US. He was urged to do so by his friend, the editor Carl Weissner, who had published his books in Germany. But the most memorable experience came in Andernach, where he met his mother's brother, Heinrich Fett, who was 90 years old.

Mannheim, 1978 —

Although the journey was stressful, Hank flew to Europe again in October 1978. He had been invited to appear on the TV show 'Apostrophes', organised by Bernard Pivot, who had a major influence on the European cultural scene, promoting the careers of new writers. Also, of course, Bukowski wanted to get to know Paris.

Everything seemed to go wrong. He turned up drunk at the studio and provoked the presenter by offering him a drink in front of the cameras. He behaved in the old, ill-mannered, iconoclastic way: he noticeably stroked the leg of a female writer sitting next to him; he got bored with listening to the other guests, who would not let him speak, and, in one of the most memorable moments in French TV history, he suddenly got up, tore out his earpiece and walked off the set mumbling to himself. The next day, he said he could remember nothing about what had happened, but he later wrote that he was irritated by the presence in the studio of a 'shrink who had given the shock treatments' to the French writer Antonin Artaud.

When a security guard tried to calm him down on his way out, Hank pulled out a knife, but he was quickly subdued. Meanwhile, Pivot went on air to tell viewers that Bukowski's behaviour showed the decadence of American literature.

I'm supposed to be the last specimen of an extinct species.

Hank's behaviour turned out to be a master stroke. In France, Pivot was seen as a star. But the media also wrote up Bukowski's performance as the most fitting attitude that a cultural agitator could adopt. Sales of his books rocketed in France. Critics dubbed him the last of the Beatniks, and this, naturally, infuriated Bukowski.

Throughout the fifties I was drunk, and I detest all that bohemian Greenwich Village, Parisian bullshit. Algiers, Tangiers... that's all romantic claptrap. I feel more like a punk than a Beatnik.

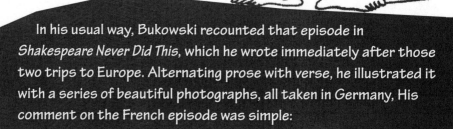

In his usual way, Bukowski recounted that episode in *Shakespeare Never Did This*, which he wrote immediately after those two trips to Europe. Alternating prose with verse, he illustrated it with a series of beautiful photographs, all taken in Germany, His comment on the French episode was simple:

I get like that when I'm drinking...

Shakespeare never did this

9 A Taste of Honey Then the Knife

Hank began the eighties with another novel, *Ham on Rye* (1982). Now the journey into the past went as far back as possible; gone were all the years of wandering from city to city, of insane drudgery, of licentiousness. Hank now explored his own earliest years, as one of his favourite writers, William Saroyan, had done in *The Human Comedy*.

The radical difference was that those were in no sense golden years, but the very darkest. Everything that Henry Chinaski had been for readers of *Post Office*, *Factotum* and *Women*, was explained to a great extent in *Ham on Rye*.

In this novel, for the first time, Bukowski's years of real terror, from childhood to adolescence, came to the surface.

Most teachers didn't trust or like me, especially the lady teachers. I never said anything out of the way but they claimed it was my 'attitude'. It was something about the way I sat slouched in my seat and my 'voice tone'. I was usually accused of 'sneering' although I wasn't conscious of it. The principal always did the same thing. He had a phone booth in his office. He made me stand in the phone booth with the door closed. I spent many hours in that phone booth. The only reading material in there was the Ladies Home Journal. It was deliberate torture. I read the Ladies Home Journal anyhow. I got to read each new issue. I hoped that maybe I could learn something about women.

In these writings, there was scarcely any hope. He saw the future 'through a glass darkly'. In his view, the eighties were a kind of re-run of the thirties.

If childhood had been painful and old age empty, and the rest just resignation... what else was there? Hank seemed to have only one response: to keep on telling and telling, and above all to add a bit of humour. And he was always ready for the next drink, when everything mattered less.

the proud thin dying

**I see old people on pensions in the
supermarkets and they are thin and they are
proud and they are dying
they are starving on their feet and saying
nothing...**

**...they'll die without a sound
pulled out of roominghouses
by young blond boys with long hair
who'll slide them in
and pull away from the curb...**

**...it's the order of things: each one
gets a taste of honey
then the knife.**

One of Hank's friends and admirers, the poet and writer Neeli Cherkovski, felt that Hank's life, as randomly recorded in his four novels, deserved to be put into some kind of order in a new critical work. Cherkovski asked:

Cherkovski and Bukowski had known each other since the 1960s. By 1983 they had not met for six years. So, after a series of conversations with Hank, Cherkovski embarked upon a task that would take another six years: to write a kind of authorised biography, based on, but not limited to, his literary work.

Hank, The Life of Charles Bukowski (1991) did not only set the record straight, it also gave an overall picture of the development of the city of Los Angeles in the twentieth century. The biographer wrote:

In understanding his life, it is crucial to come to grips with the place he has chosen as his home. Few writers have given themselves over to the immediate world around them so completely as has Bukowski. His skill lies in taking his environment, his city, and making it universal. The particular place becomes the human city everywhere.

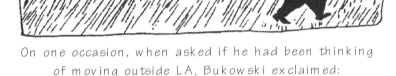

On one occasion, when asked if he had been thinking of moving outside LA, Bukowski exclaimed:

Nevertheless, the choice of San Pedro for his home had moved him from the centre of the LA scene. That new life, away from the hustle and bustle, brought new elements into his verse: birds, for example. The poems, without being less descriptive, became in some ways more philosophical. Hank had grown old and he became preoccupied with the theme of the passage of time, the slow, inexorable cycle. It could be said that his basic ideology, that of a tough, sardonic man, had been tempered, over the years, by a dash of melancholy, a lyrical concession which made him a more attractive personality. 'The Mockingbird', for instance, tells of the bird mocking a cat throughout the summer, until finally, the cat achieves its revenge and clasps the bird in its mouth:

The Mockingbird

...and the bird was no longer mocking,
it was asking, it was praying
but the cat
striding down through centuries
would not listen

Based partly on interviews with the writer, Cherkovski's *Hank* shed light on some episodes that seemed merely amusing—or written solely from Hank's point of view—in various works, like the famous 'postal' marriage. Conceived out of admiration for Bukowski, and almost like a novel itself, the biography opens on a sunny spring day in 1926, with Hank as a small boy about to disobey his father and go to play ball down the street...

...and it ends with Hank as an old man driving a black BMW through a maze of intersections so as to get to work on his computer.

When Neeli Cherkovski met up with Hank again in 1983, Bukowski had become an internationally-renowned writer. On his bookshelves were his own works translated into German, Italian, French, Dutch, Norwegian and Spanish, among other languages.

It was then that the Italian director Marco Ferreri made a feature film, *Tales of Ordinary Madness*, with Ben Gazzara and Ornella Mutti, based on his fiction. Hank did not like the style. Soon after, the Belgian director Dominique Deruddere made a film, *Crazy Love (Love is a Dog from Hell)*, centred around some of his stories. Bukowski did like this film, believing it to be a more accurate portrayal.

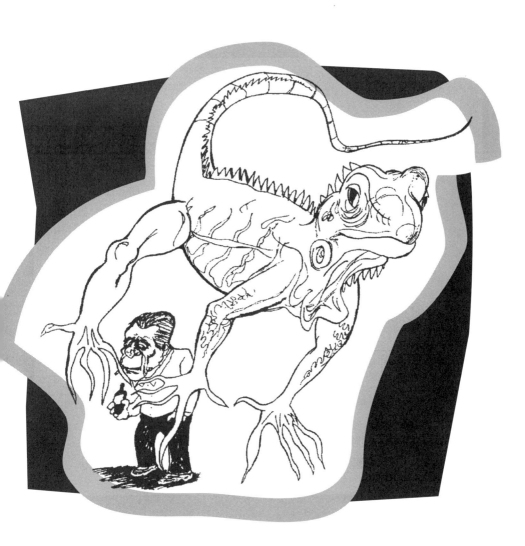

Fernanda Pivano's book was one indication that the former 'Dirty Old Man' had achieved international recognition. During the three-hour interview, Hank responded good humouredly to odd questions of all kinds.

That itself was strange since he detested reporters. He felt defenceless before journalists and that brought back the shyness of his earlier years. Still, he was adept enough at lying to elicit a kind of intimacy which was apparent whenever some of his wilder excesses appeared in print.

At one point, Pivano questioned him about the amount of money he had made and the opportunities it had opened up for him. She suggested that his lifestyle must have become diametrically opposed to that depicted in his narrative work up until then.

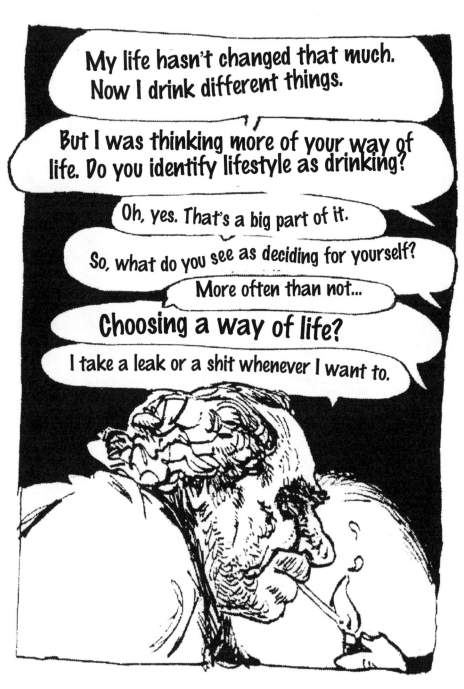

But you can't ignore the need to have a shit, just as you can't ignore....

...neither can I ignore drinking. I'd die if I gave up doing either! You know? In one way or another I'd be dead. Do I drink when I write or do I write when I drink? You understand.

Yes.

And writing is ninety per cent of myself. The other ten is hoping, waiting to be able to write.

The phrase 'I drink *different things*' was, in its way, an acknowledgement of Linda's influence. Apart from administering a daily cocktail of vitamins, she had convinced him to give up the hard stuff, like whisky and vodka, in favour of good quality wines.

Linda pointed out that wine was lower in alcohol. Doctors had told her that a change in his drinking habits would lessen the headstrong old man's suffering and susceptibility to illness.

Hank had recovered from the ulcer that had landed him in hospital at age 36. But he was nursing the leukemia that would eventually kill him.

My favourite wine is a homage to my native Germany: white Rhine wine.

Complications arising from Bukowski's ill-health and the exhausting after-effects of notoriety did not distract him from his creative work. *Hot Water Music*, yet another book of short stories came out in 1983 and the next year, there was a collection of recent verse, *War All the Time: Poems 1981-4*.

Extensive work followed on the script for *Barfly*. Hank took part in the filming and built a good relationship with the cast, which kept him occupied for a long period, but it soon became clear that he was up to his old tricks—living his life so as to tell it all to his readers.

In order to persuade Hank to take part in his film, Barbet Schroeder had had to call upon all manner of resources ranging from flattery to physical threats.

Many people who got involved with Hank during those years were unprepared. They believed that he wrote only about the past. They were mistaken. They too would become material for his writing. Hank's affair with Hollywood, with no concessions made to commercial strategies, had an unexpected effect: many in the media who until then had criticised him came to praise him instead.

On 22 March 1987, the *Los Angeles Times* published an article by Paul Ciotto, devoted to Bukowski. It was illustrated with a series of photographs, one of which showed the Bukowskis posing in front of their home, flanked by two powerful automobiles. Neeli Cherkovski could imagine...

10 Hollywood

In May 1988, Bukowski fell ill with tuberculosis and had to give up drinking for what seemed to him quite some time—and he succeeded until the day of Marina's wedding in October of that year. That over, he started on his fifth novel *Hollywood* which was published in 1989.

Those of his fans who thought that Hank had changed for the worse by becoming rich and famous could set their minds at rest.

The novel was a depiction of his new life, with the filming of *Barfly* as the trigger. It was another case of settling old scores, but this time with the banal and artificial world of movies. The script had portrayed just a few years of his life, but now he added fictional characters based on the main members of the cast, the director and his army of co-workers and even the production executives. Of course, he changed their names, as he had always done with the subjects of his fiction. *Hollywood* includes a conversation with Faye Dunaway, whom he renamed Francine (he described her as taking notes, like a student, of the things he had said), and Mickey Rourke whom he called Rick Talbot. Linda was also included in the conversation, as a woman called Sarah. It is interesting to note the setting of this work; the loser has turned into a winner, into a guru whose shrine is visited by Hollywood stars. But his view of them continues to reveal a sarcasm that is at times merciless.

'Listen, Hank, I want to know some
more about Jane. Indian, right?'

'Half-Indian, half-Irish.'

'Why did she drink?'

'It was a place to hide and also
a slow form of suicide.'

131

Celebrities like Madonna, her then husband Sean Penn (who was such a fan that he would have given his right arm to be in *Barfly*), Dennis Hopper, and Harry Dean Stanton used to visit San Pedro. They all wanted to find out if the old legend was really so tough.

Bukowski did not spare them his hurtful and bad-tempered comments, but that only delighted them even more. That was partly what they had come for.

In chapter 37 of *Hollywood* which opens with a glitzy photo call for Francine, the author elaborates on the feelings awakened by the world of movies:

Then everybody just walked off and Sarah and I walked into the bar. The regular barflies were there. They were movie stars now and had developed a certain dignity. They had become quieter, as if thinking about great things. I liked them better the old way.

rubber skinned man

hunchback midget

lucy jones

the man with two faces

Sarah and I were taking it easy. I ordered a beer and she had a red wine.

11 An Old Writer with a Yellow Notebook

Hank's relapse in 1988 had turned out to be an omen, warning that, although he had survived, his days were numbered. Now in his seventies, he faced the physical decline with the same stubborn energy that had kept him going all along. He wrote until he could no longer. His thoughts turned to Linda and he worried about:

my wife left with
this pile of nothing
Confessions

...and he laughed at the sorrowful faces around him. Some of the poems he was then writing centred almost obsessively around the theme of health.

Some of Bukowski's last poems focus on physical decline with a mixture of the old grumpy humour and a new feeling of satisfaction faced with the inevitable.

...my typewriter is
my tombstone
still

and I am
reduced to bird
watching...

8 Count

...there's a bluebird in my heart that
wants to get out
but I pour whiskey on him and inhale
cigarette smoke...

Bluebird

Cornered

now
my once-promise
dwindling
dwindling

now
lighting new cigarettes
pouring more
drinks

it has been a beautiful
fight

still
is.

BUKOWSKI

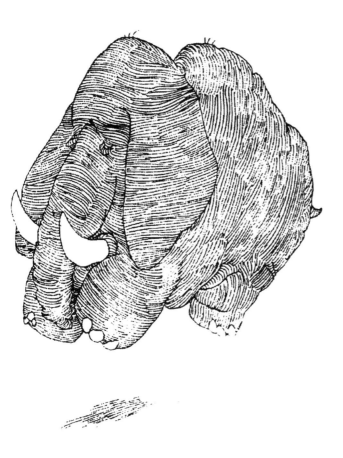

Two years before his death, his friend and publisher John Martin had hoped to raise Bukowski's spirits by offering him a project that would build on Cherkovski's work. It would fill out the biography by concentrating solely on the published work. Martin had known Bukowski intimately for 25 years. What he proposed was to organise the best autobiographical texts in chronological order, so as to compile an authentic book of memoirs.

Run with the Hunted, which appeared in 1993, subtly interweaved material taken from more than twenty of Bukowski's books. It was a work which was clearly a tribute to the author's consistency of style. For those who had not read Bukowski, the book was an invaluable guide to his work, which was also his life.

But, although sick, Hank could not allow the last book of his life to be John Martin's. His swansong would be a novel, the shortest and the most praised of the six he had written. *Pulp*, edited after his death, had a new and powerful element: the protagonist was no longer Henry Chinaski. Hank had invented a detective in the mould of Philip Marlowe, but he would remain forever bound to his alter ego.

Pulp (1994) is a parody of cheap detective fiction. It shows the private detective, Nick Belane, in a series of linked adventures in the setting of contemporary LA. Belane is 55, with three costly divorces behind him, a neighbour whom he cannot stand (who is a postman), and he is on the verge of alcoholism. One of his main adversaries is himself, in his infinite despair.

He has to track down the Red Sparrow—a play on the Maltese Falcon. He contends with voluptuous extra-terrestrials and with Lady Death, in person. He meets the ghost of Louis-Ferdinand Céline, and, above all he has to put up with himself, down and out and cocky.

Bukowski was not mocking Raymond Chandler, that other great voice of the city. Rather, he was paying homage to him as an old comrade who also lacked academic recognition. The choice of a style that was a minor genre, according to academics, was a way of dealing with some kind of finality. Chandler, that other explorer of the dark side of the city of illusions, had set out to publish his stories in magazines printed on ordinary woodpulp or newsprint, so as to be the cheapest on the market. Therefore, by extension, the term 'pulp' was used to describe a certain kind of detec-tive novel.

bukowski's music

Hank had all of that spinning in his head when he was writing, knowing that death awaited him. The French critic Liliane Kerjan said of *Pulp*:

'A journey to the remains of the day, dead for a fistful of dollars, a ridiculous search for the holy grail. In his G&T style, Bukowski revisits the nightmare areas of American society—violence, consumerism, funeral processions and television. Plus the waiting rooms outside the attorney's or psychiatrist's office with their rejected and interchangeable clients. A fascinating homage to literature and the darkest possible lives...'

In the twists of the plot, in surreal moments, readers can tune in to the wavelength of this private detective whose philosophy is very similar to that of Chinaski, who, as in a film, has a cameo role in the novel. In a speech from *Pulp*, written in the first person, Bukowski says:

I walked toward Red's feeling a bit depressed. Man was born to die. What did it mean? Hanging around and waiting. Waiting for the 'A train'. Waiting for a pair of big breasts on some August night in a Vegas hotel room. Waiting for the mouse to sing. Waiting for the snake to grow wings. Hanging around.

But Hank at 70 could not bear the tragedy of existence without finding some humour in it. As a writer he always saw the funny side of events, even when they were tragic. The main character, for example, describes his life in this way:

I needed a vacation. I needed 5 women. I needed to get the wax out of my ears. My car needed an oil change. I'd failed to file my damned income tax. One of the stems had broken off of my reading glasses. There were ants in my apartment. I needed to get my teeth cleaned. My shoes were run down at the heels.

In this book, Bukowski shows his love of literature in a way that has no precedent in his previous work. What he is saying becomes less important than how he says it and, for the first time, a more gentle humour envelops the story.

I hadn't laughed in 6 years. I tended to worry when there was nothing to worry about. And when there was something to worry about, I got drunk.

Charles Bukowski died on 9 March 1994 in a hospital at San Pedro. He was 73.

ILL

being very ill and very weak is a very strange
thing.
when it takes all your strength to get from the
bedroom to the bathroom and back, it seems like
a joke but
you don't laugh.

back in bed you consider death again and find
the same thing: the closer you get to it
the less forbidding it
becomes.

In an interview with *Transit* magazine earlier in 1994, Bukowski had predicted:

If I stop writing I am dead. And that's the only way I'll stop: dead.

As often happens to great men, Bukowski died more famous for his personality than for his work. His narrative writings have been translated more often than his verse and so in many parts of the world his readers know him best as a storyteller and novelist.

The public takes from a writer, or a writing, what it needs, and lets the remainder go. But what they take is usually what they need least and what they let go is what they need most.

Do not write to save the world. I wrote to save you.

Advice of this kind might survive, stuck on the study walls
of thousands of writers throughout the world,
or engraved on their memories along with Bukowski's
undoubted influence on thousands of young writers.

Bukowski *once said* 'I **am 93 percent the person I present in my poems; the other 7 percent is where art improves upon life, call it background music.'** How much of that 93 percent was Dirty Old Man or genius, myth or reality, bravado or brutal honesty, his reader must decide.

INDEX

BIBLIOGRAPHY

BOOKS BY CHARLES BUKOWSKI

Novels

Post Office, Black Sparrow Press, 1970

Factotum, Black Sparrow Press, 1975

Women, Black Sparrow Press, 1978

Ham on Rye, Black Sparrow Press, 1982

Hollywood, Black Sparrow Press, 1989

Pulp, Black Sparrow Press, 1994

Poetry

Flower, Fist and Bestial Wail, Hearse Press, 1960

Longshot Pomes for Broke Players, 7 Poets Press, 1962

Run With the Hunted, Midwest Press, 1962

It Catches My Heart in Its Hands, Loujon Press, 1963

Crucifix in a Deathhand, Loujon Press, 1965

Cold Dogs in the Courtyard, Literary Times-Cyfoeth, 1965

The Genius of the Crowd, 7 Flower Press, 1966

At Terror Street and Agony Way, Black Sparrow Press, 1968

Poems Written Before Jumping out of an 8 Story Window, Poetry X / Change/ Litmus,
  1968

The Days Run Away Like Wild Horses Over the Hills, Black Sparrow Press, 1969

Mockingbird Wish Me Luck, Black Sparrow Press, 1970

Burning in Water Drowning in Flame: Selected Poems 1955-1973, Black Sparrow Press,
  1974

Love is a Dog from Hell: Poems 1974-77, Black Sparrow Press, 1977

Play the Piano Drunk Like a Percussion Instrument Until the Fingers Begin to Bleed a Bit, Black
  Sparrow Press, 1979

Dangling in the Tournefortia, Black Sparrow Press, 1981

War All the Time: Poems 1981-84, Black Sparrow Press, 1984

You Get So Alone at Times That It Just Makes Sense, Black Sparrow Press, 1986

The Roominghouse Madrigals: Early Selected Poems 1946-1966, Black Sparrow Press,
  1988

The Last Night of the Earth Poems, Black Sparrow Press, 1992

Bone Palace Ballet: New Poems, Black Sparrow Press, 1997

Prose

Confessions of a Man Insane Enough To Live with Beasts, Ole Press, 1965

All the Assholes in the World and Mine, Ole Press, 1966

Notes of a Dirty Old Man, Essex House, 1969

Erections, Ejaculations, Exhibitions and General Tales of Ordinary Madness, City Lights Books, 1972

The Most Beautiful Woman in the World, City Lights Books, 1983

Tales of Ordinary Madness, City Lights Books, 1983

South of No North, Black Sparrow Press, 1973

Hot Water Music, Black Sparrow Press, 1983

Screams From the Balcony: Selected Letters, 1960-1970, Black Sparrow Press, 1993

Living on Luck: Selected Letters, 1960s-1970s, Black Sparrow Press, 1995

Poetry & Prose

Shakespeare Never Did This, City Lights Books, 1979

Septuagenarian Stew, Black Sparrow Press, 1990

Run With the Hunted: A Charles Bukowski Reader, Harper & Row, 1993

Betting on the Muse: Poems and Short Stories, Black Sparrow Press, 1996

Film Script

The Movie: 'Barfly', Black Sparrow Press, 1987

BOOKS ABOUT CHARLES BUKOWSKI

Brewer, Gay, *Charles Bukowski*, Twaynes United States Authors Series, 1997

Cherkovski, Neeli, *Hank: the Life of Charles Bukowski*, Random House, 1991

Christy, Jim, *The Buk Book*, ECW Press, 1997

Fox, Hugh, *Charles Bukowski: A Critical and Bibliographical Study*, Abyss Publications, 1969

Harrison, Russell, *Against the American Dream: Essays on Charles Bukowski*, Black Sparrow Press, 1994

Locklin, Gerald, *Charles Bukowski: A Sure Bet*, Water Row Press, 1996

Richmond, Steve, *Spinning Off Bukowski*, Sun Dog Press, 1996

Sherman, Jory, *Bukowski: Friendship, Fame and Bestial Myth*, Blue Horse Publications, 1981

Sounes, Howard:, *Charles Bukowski: Locked in the Arms of a Crazy Life* Rebel Inc., 1998

Winans, A.D., *The Charles Bukowski Flash, Second Coming Years*, Beat Scene Press, 1996

THE FOR BEGINNERS® SERIES

AFRICAN HISTORY FOR BEGINNERS: ISBN 978-1-934389-18-8

ANARCHISM FOR BEGINNERS: ISBN 978-1-934389-32-4

ARABS & ISRAEL FOR BEGINNERS: ISBN 978-1-934389-16-4

ART THEORY FOR BEGINNERS: ISBN 978-1-934389-47-8

ASTRONOMY FOR BEGINNERS: ISBN 978-1-934389-25-6

AYN RAND FOR BEGINNERS: ISBN 978-1-934389-37-9

BARACK OBAMA FOR BEGINNERS, AN ESSENTIAL GUIDE: ISBN 978-1-934389-44-7

BEN FRANKLIN FOR BEGINNERS: ISBN 978-1-934389-48-5

BLACK HISTORY FOR BEGINNERS: ISBN 978-1-934389-19-5

THE BLACK HOLOCAUST FOR BEGINNERS: ISBN 978-1-934389-03-4

BLACK WOMEN FOR BEGINNERS: ISBN 978-1-934389-20-1

CHOMSKY FOR BEGINNERS: ISBN 978-1-934389-17-1

DADA & SURREALISM FOR BEGINNERS: ISBN 978-1-934389-00-3

DANTE FOR BEGINNERS: ISBN 978-1-934389-67-6

DECONSTRUCTION FOR BEGINNERS: ISBN 978-1-934389-26-3

DEMOCRACY FOR BEGINNERS: ISBN 978-1-934389-36-2

DERRIDA FOR BEGINNERS: ISBN 978-1-934389-11-9

EASTERN PHILOSOPHY FOR BEGINNERS: ISBN 978-1-934389-07-2

EXISTENTIALISM FOR BEGINNERS: ISBN 978-1-934389-21-8

FANON FOR BEGINNERS ISBN 978-1-934389-87-4

FDR AND THE NEW DEAL FOR BEGINNERS: ISBN 978-1-934389-50-8

FOUCAULT FOR BEGINNERS: ISBN 978-1-934389-12-6

FRENCH REVOLUTIONS FOR BEGINNERS: ISBN 978-1-934389-91-1

GENDER & SEXUALITY FOR BEGINNERS: ISBN 978-1-934389-69-0

GLOBAL WARMING FOR BEGINNERS: ISBN 978-1-934389-27-0

GREEK MYTHOLOGY FOR BEGINNERS: ISBN 978-1-934389-83-6

HEIDEGGER FOR BEGINNERS: ISBN 978-1-934389-13-3

THE HISTORY OF CLASSICAL MUSIC FOR BEGINNERS: ISBN 978-1-939994-26-4

THE HISTORY OF OPERA FOR BEGINNERS: ISBN 978-1-934389-79-9

ISLAM FOR BEGINNERS: ISBN 978-1-934389-01-0

JANE AUSTEN FOR BEGINNERS: ISBN 978-1-934389-61-4

JUNG FOR BEGINNERS: ISBN 978-1-934389-76-8

KIERKEGAARD FOR BEGINNERS: ISBN 978-1-934389-14-0

LACAN FOR BEGINNERS: ISBN 978-1-934389-39-3

LINCOLN FOR BEGINNERS: ISBN 978-1-934389-85-0

LINGUISTICS FOR BEGINNERS: ISBN 978-1-934389-28-7

MALCOLM X FOR BEGINNERS: ISBN 978-1-934389-04-1

MARX'S *DAS KAPITAL* FOR BEGINNERS: ISBN 978-1-934389-59-1

MCLUHAN FOR BEGINNERS: ISBN 978-1-934389-75-1

NIETZSCHE FOR BEGINNERS: ISBN 978-1-934389-05-8

PAUL ROBESON FOR BEGINNERS ISBN 978-1-934389-81-2

PHILOSOPHY FOR BEGINNERS: ISBN 978-1-934389-02-7

PLATO FOR BEGINNERS: ISBN 978-1-934389-08-9

POETRY FOR BEGINNERS: ISBN 978-1-934389-46-1

POSTMODERNISM FOR BEGINNERS: ISBN 978-1-934389-09-6

RELATIVITY & QUANTUM PHYSICS FOR BEGINNERS: ISBN 978-1-934389-42-3

SARTRE FOR BEGINNERS: ISBN 978-1-934389-15-7

SHAKESPEARE FOR BEGINNERS: ISBN 978-1-934389-29-4

STANISLAVSKI FOR BEGINNERS ISBN 978-1-939994-35-6

STRUCTURALISM & POSTSTRUCTURALISM FOR BEGINNERS: ISBN 978-1-934389-10-2

WOMEN'S HISTORY FOR BEGINNERS: ISBN 978-1-934389-60-7

UNIONS FOR BEGINNERS: ISBN 978-1-934389-77-5

U.S. CONSTITUTION FOR BEGINNERS: ISBN 978-1-934389-62-1

ZEN FOR BEGINNERS: ISBN 978-1-934389-06-5

ZINN FOR BEGINNERS: ISBN 978-1-934389-40-9

www.forbeginnersbooks.com